Love & Kisses

A Light Heart...
f...

There was a young lady from Gloucester,
Whose boyfriend thought he had lost her;
From the fridge came a sound,
At last she was found,
The problem was how to defrost her.

Other joke books from
Methuen Children's Books

The Green and Hairy Joke Book – Gus Berry

My Funny Valentine – Katie Wales

MARTYN FORRESTER

Love & Kisses

A Light Hearted Book for your Valentine

From your Secret Admirer xxx

Methuen Children's Books

First published as a Methuen Children's Book
paperback original in 1989
by Methuen Children's Books
A Division of the Octopus Group Ltd
Michelin House, 81 Fulham Road, London SW3 6RB
Text copyright © 1989 Martyn Forrester
Illustrations copyright © 1989 Mark Burgess
Printed and bound in Great Britain
by Cox & Wyman

Forrester, Martyn, 1952–
Love and kisses: a light hearted book
for your valentine.
I. Title
828'.91409

ISBN 0–416–13632–X

Roses are red,
Violets are blue,
Guess who's so sweet
They bought this book for you?

The Story of St Valentine's Day

Long before St Valentine was made the
patron saint of courtship and love, the
ancient Romans held a festival during
February in honour of their great god Pan.
The festival was called Lupercalia, and
one of its most important customs was for
the names of young women and men to be
placed in a box and then drawn out – a bit
like a raffle or the FA Cup draw – to match
up pairs of token sweethearts.

Much later, and still in Rome, there lived a Catholic priest called Valentine. It was the third century AD, a time when the emperor, Claudius, had banned marriage because he thought it prevented men from making good soldiers. Valentine, however, performed secret wedding ceremonies for lovers who wanted to be married. He was caught, and brutally murdered – on the eve of the feast of Lupercalia.

To this day, 14th February is dedicated to his memory.

Many superstitions and customs have grown up around this special day. For example, it is believed that the first person you see when you wake up on 14th February will be your Valentine, so bad luck if it's the family dog.

If you put sweet-smelling flowers under your pillow the night before, it's said you will dream of your future partner. Put a cauliflower under your pillow and you won't even get to sleep in the first place.

Since the Middle Ages, lovers have sent each other flowers and presents on St Valentine's Day, but it was the Victorians who started sending Valentine cards with lovehearts, flowers and lace on the outside, and romantic poems on the inside. Sometimes the cards were also decorated with birds, because of an old belief that birds chose their mates on this day for spring nesting:

You'll be mine and I'll be thine,
And so good-morrow Valentine;
As I sat in my garden chair,
I saw two birds fly in the air;
And two by two and pair by pair,
Which made me think of you, my dear.

If you see a sparrow on St Valentine's Day you will soon be marrying a farmer. If you see a robin, you will soon be wed to a sailor. And if you see a pink pterodactyl flying upside down singing God Save The Queen, you will soon be seeing a psychiatrist.

Roses are red.
Violets are blue.
Orchids are expensive,
Will dandelions do?

Valentine Fax

On February 14th, 1929, members of Al
Capone's gang dressed up as policemen
and killed seven unarmed men belonging
to 'Bugs' Moran's rival bunch of villains.
The event became known as the St
Valentine's Day Massacre.

Knock, Knock

Knock, knock.
– Who's there?
Murray.
– Murray who?
Murray me? Not likely?

Knock, knock.
– Who's there?
Percy.
– Percy who?
Percy Vere and she'll say yes!

Monster Kisses

What happened when Romeo Ghost met
Juliet Ghost?
It was love at first fright.

Why should you be careful of beautiful
witches?
Because they'll sweep you off your feet.

Who did the monster marry?
His ghoulfriend.

Why did the girl marry the ghost?
She didn't know what possessed her.

What do you call a pretty ghost?
Boooo-tiful!

What did the hippy ghost say to his
girlfriend?
'Hey girl, you're really out of sight . . .'

What did the hippy ghost's girlfriend
reply?
'Real ghoul, man . . .'

What did the ghost say to his girlfriend on
their second date?
'It's nice not to see you again.'

Did you hear about the two unmarried ghosts who lived together?
They believed in doing what comes supernaturally.

Why do demons and ghouls get on so well?
Because demons are a ghoul's best friend.

What kind of dates do ghouls go out with?
Anyone they can dig up.

What famous play about ghosts in love was written by William Shakespeare?
Romeo and Ghouliet.

What does a female bride throw to her bridesmaids at her wedding?
Her boooo-quet!

Why wasn't the ghost very popular with
the girls at parties?
He wasn't very much to look at.

What did the boy skeleton say to the girl
skeleton?
'I love every bone in your body.'

A St Valentine's Day Puzzle

Can you turn the word ROSE into the word LOVE in just four moves, changing only one letter each time?

ROSE

. . . .

. . . .

LOVE

(Answer: ROSE
          DOSE
          DOVE
          LOVE)

From the Romantic Bookshelf . . .

* My Golden Wedding by Annie Versary

* When Shall We Meet Again? by
Miles Apart

* The Jilted Lover by I. Malone

* Make Yourself More Attractive by
A. Magnet

* Our Date is Over by Olga Home

* A Disease Called Love by Willie Catchit

* A Kiss At Christmas by Miss L. Toe

* Mad About You by Cy Deeply

* The Weekend Bride by Marion Sunday

* The proposal by Mary Mee

* Adam and Eve by Gordon F. Eden

* The Girl With The Hard Heart by
Mada Stone

* Popping The Question by
Jemima R. Sking

* How To Look Attractive by May Cup

Roses are red,
Violets are blue,
Don't call us,
We'll call you!

Valentine Nicknames

Some people don't send Valentine cards any more, they put announcements in the newspapers instead. That gives the rest of us the chance to find out all the amazing names that lovers call each other. So if you're stuck for a nickname for your loved name, why not borrow one from this year's list?

Fattyburger
Jellybaby
Mr Polar Bear
Silly Goose
Skunkworks
Slapper
Squashy
Squidgims
Sticky Sheep

Sweetpea
Tabitha Twitchit
Ratbag
Burglar's Cat
Tinkerboo
Schnook
Snugglebee
Strumper
Toady

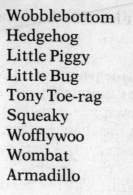

Wobblebottom
Hedgehog
Little Piggy
Little Bug
Tony Toe-rag
Squeaky
Wofflywoo
Wombat
Armadillo

Bumblecluck
Bumpkin
Bugalugs
Big Ears
Blobby
Boffin Babes
Scabby Rat
Snugglebum
Werewolf

Snugglebug Smurf
Smelly Moose
Kissyface
Kitty Molehill
Lollipop
Marsupial
Moonface
Moosey Poo
Karen Kitten

Maltese Falcon
Golden Face
Miss Piggy
Rupert Bear
Podgy Squirrel
Puggles
Badger
Chocolate Buttons
Mango Monster
Dumbo

♡ ✕ ♡ ✕ ♡ ✕ ♡ ✕ ♡ ✕ ♡ ♡ ✕ ♡ ✕ ♡ ♡ ✕ ♡ ✕ ♡

Romantic Tip No 1

You know it's not going to be a good St Valentine's Day when the only card you get is addressed: Dear Occupant . . .

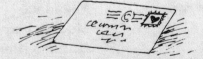

Roses are red,
Violets are blue.
But who needs flowers
When I've got you?

Knock, Knock Again

Knock, knock.
– Who's there?
Kipper.
– Kipper who?
Kipper hands to yourself.

Knock, knock.
– Who's there?
Wooden Shoe.
– Wooden Shoe who?
Wooden Shoe like to know who sent you
your Valentine?

Romance at the St Valentine's Disco

BOY: Until I met you, life was just one big desert.
GIRL: Is that why you dance like a camel?

BOY: You would be a great dancer except for two things.
GIRL: What are they?
BOY: Your feet!

GIRL: Darling, I want to dance like this forever.
BOY: Don't you ever want to improve?

BOY: I never danced so badly before.
GIRL: Oh, then you have danced before?

BOY: May I have the last dance?
GIRL: You've just had it.

BOY: I love you and I could die for you!
GIRL: How soon?

BOY: Would you marry the biggest idiot on earth?
GIRL: Oh Fred, that comes so sudden!

GIRL: I love men who are frank.
BOY: Too bad, my name is Jonathon.

GIRL: The moment you kissed me I knew
it was puppy love.
BOY: Why was that?
GIRL: Your nose was cold.

GIRL: Do you ever think of me?
BOY: Yes, but I'd hate to tell you what.

BOY: What would you say if I asked you to
marry me?
GIRL: Nothing. I can't talk and laugh at
the same time.

BOY: I would go to the end of the earth for
you!
GIRL: Yes, but would you stay there?

BOY: Are you fond of nuts?
GIRL: Is this a proposal?

BOY: May I see you pretty soon?
GIRL: Don't you think I'm pretty now?

BOY TO GIRLFRIEND: Darling you look wonderful – what happened?

GIRL: What has she got that I haven't got?
BOY: Shall I give it to you alphabetically?

BOY: Darling, the whole world revolves around you.
GIRL: Well, I told you not to drink that glass of beer!

GIRL: Where did you get those big eyes?
BOY: They came with the face.

BOY TO GIRLFRIEND: I'd like to run my fingers through your hair. Can you remember where you left it?

SISTER: Jack is the sweetest, most darling husband in all the world.
BROTHER: Too bad you married George.

GIRL: If you were my husband I'd give you poison.
BOY: If you were my wife I'd take it.

BOY: I love you terribly.
GIRL: You certainly do.

1ST BOY: My girlfriend has beautiful hair.
2ND BOY: Mine too. Every time we go out I insist that she wears it.

BOY: There are times when I really like you.
GIRL: When is that?
BOY: When you're not yourself!

BOY TO GIRLFRIEND: I'd like to pay you a compliment . . . but I can't think of one.

BOY: Since we met, I can't eat or drink.
GIRL: Why not?
BOY: I'm broke!

GIRL AT CINEMA: I love you so much I've
got a cold, slithery feeling down my neck.
BOY: So that's where my Cornetto went!

BOY: Oh darling, what would it take to make you give me a kiss?
GIRL: An anaesthetic.

BOY: Looks aren't everything.
GIRL: In your case they aren't anything.

1ST GIRL: What about Danny? What do you think of his looks?
2ND GIRL: I don't mind him looking – it's his face I can't stand!

BOY: I can't leave you.
GIRL: Do you love me so much?
BOY: It's not that. You're standing on my foot.

SHARON: Have you ever had a hot, passionate, burning kiss?
TRACY: I did once. He'd forgotten to take the cigarette out of his mouth.

GIRL: Do you think I'll lose my looks as I get older?
BOY: With a bit of luck, yes.

BARBARA: Do you love me?
BOY: I would die for you.
BARBARA: You're always saying that but you never do it.

PENNY: You remind me of my favourite boxer.

BOB: Frank Bruno? Barry McGuigan?

PENNY: No. I think he's called Rover.

BOY: You look like an Italian dish.

GIRL: Madonna? Sophia Loren?

BOY: No, macaroni cheese.

BOY: May I hold your hand?

GIRL: No thanks, it isn't heavy.

GIRL: Did you miss me while I was away?

BOY: Were you away?

GIRL: How do you like me?

BOY: As girls go, you're fine. And the sooner you go, the better.

BOY: I've been told I have an infectious smile.

GIRL: In that case, don't stand too close to me.

Valentine Fax

People from the Philippines have a really strange way of kissing – they put their lips to each other's face and inhale very quickly.

The longest screen kiss ever occurred between Regis Toomey and Jane Wyman in the 1941 film *You're in the Army Now*. Their lip-smacking marathon lasted a breathtaking three minutes!

In the film *Don Juan,* starring John Barrymore, there is on average one kiss every 53 seconds.

The first film kiss on Indian screens was not allowed until 1978.

The Chinese did not kiss until the practice was introduced by westerners. Apparently they're still not very keen on it.

Paul Trevillion and Sadie Nine established the world record for kissing in 1975 – 20,009 in two hours. It is reported that after training, Sadie managed to double the size of her lips.

The animal kingdom is not immune from the love bug. Snails kiss before mating – and male Adelie penguins present their chosen partner with a stone, which forms the foundation of their nest. If she accepts, they then stand chest to chest and sing a love song together.

Roses are red,
Violets are blue,
Sugar is sweet
And rots your teeth too.

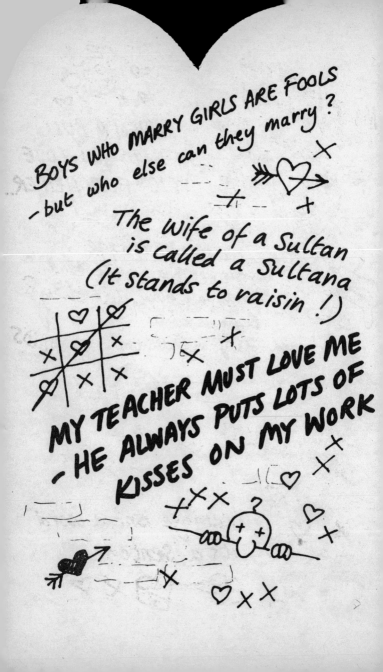

BOYS WHO MARRY GIRLS ARE FOOLS
— but who else can they marry?

The wife of a Sultan
is called a Sultana
(It stands to raisin!)

MY TEACHER MUST LOVE ME
— HE ALWAYS PUTS LOTS OF
KISSES ON MY WORK

More Knock, Knock

Knock, knock.
– Who's there?
Fanny.
– Fanny who?
Fanny boys call, say I'm out.

Knock, knock.
– Who's there?
Jimmy.
– Jimmy who?
Jimmy a little kiss on the cheek.

Knock, knock.
– Who's there?
Cereal.
– Cereal who?
Cereal pleasure to meet you.

Knock, knock.
– Who's there?
Honeydew.
– Honeydew who?
Honeydew want to come out tonight?

Knock, knock.
– Who's there?
Felix.
– Felix who?
Felix Ited about seeing you tonight

Knock, knock.
– Who's there?
Jackson.
– Jackson who?
Jackson the telephone
again, you'd better
answer it.

♥ ✕ ♥ ✕ ♥ ✕ ♥ ✕ ♥ ✕ ♥ ✕ ♥ ✕ ♥ ✕ ♥ ✕ ♥

Romantic Tip No 2

It is better to have loved a short girl than
never to have loved a tall . . .

Romantic Rhymes and Mush Verse

There was a young lady of Thrace,
Whose nose spread all over her face;
She'd very few kisses,
The reason for this is
There wasn't a suitable place.

There was a young fellow of Perth,
Who was born on the day of his birth;
He was married, they say,
On his wife's wedding day,
And he died when he quitted this earth.

The bottle of perfume that Willie sent
Was highly displeasing to Millicent;
Her thanks were so cold,
They quarrelled, I'm told,
Through the silly scent Willie sent
Millicent.

I have watched my pet rabbits at play,
And looked at my mice twice a day;
I *know* – I'm not dumb –
Where babies come from,
But why doesn't anyone say?

There was a young lady from Gloucester,
Whose boyfriend thought that he had lost
her;
From the fridge came a sound,
At last she was found,
The problem was how to defrost her.

'Twas in a restaurant they met,
Romeo and Juliet;
He had no cash to pay the debt,
So Romeo'd what Juliet.

My love is like a cabbage,
Divided into two;
The leaves I give to others,
But my heart I give to you.

A charming young singer named Hannah
Got caught in a flood in Savannah;
As she floated away,
Her boyfriend, they say,
Accompanied her on the piannah'

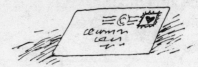

What happened when two American stoats
got married?
They become the United Stoats of
America.

What do lovesick owls say when it's
raining?
Too-wet-to-woo!

Why did the ant elope?
Nobody gnu.

What do you call two vegetables who fall
in love?
Swedehearts.

Did you hear about the idiot porcupine?
He fell in love with a scrubbing brush.

How do porcupines cuddle each other?
With great care.

Did you hear about the short-sighted
tortoise?
It fell in love with a crash helmet.

Why did the cannibal go to the wedding reception?
So that he could toast the bride.

1ST CANNIBAL WOMAN: I don't know what to make of my husband these days.
2ND CANNIBAL WOMAN: How about a nice casserole?

What is an antelope?
When two ants run away to get married.

What is the definition of romance?
Two Italian ants in love.

TREV: Who was that girl I saw you kissing
last night?
STEVE: What time was it?

Romantic Love is an itch around the heart
you cannot scratch.

'I've kissed so many girls, I can do it with
my eyes closed.'

JESSIE: Say you love me! Say you love
me!
CHARLIE: You love me!

DAVE: Tracy's got engaged to an X-ray technician.
RICK: I wonder what he sees in her?

DIANA: If we become engaged will you give me a ring?
NICK: Sure, what's your phone number?

What do you call spiders on honeymoon?
Newly-webs.

What do Boy Scouts give Girl Guides on St Valentine's Day?
Forget-me-knots.

What do squirrels give each other on St Valentine's Day?
Forget-me-nuts.

Did you hear about the two elephants who fell in love?
They sent each other mammoth Valentine cards.

How do bats find each other in the dark?
Delightful!

How to Murmur Sweet Nothings in Lots of Different Countries

(Not to Mention Lots of Different Ears!)

ENGLISH: Honeybunch.
FRENCH: Mon petit chou à la crème.
GERMAN: Affenschwanzchen.
ITALIAN: Dolce trescoro.
SPANISH: Cachito de liel.

ENGLISH:	Beautiful.
FRENCH:	Belle.
GERMAN:	Schon.
ITALIAN:	Bella.
SPANISH:	Hermosa.

ENGLISH:	True love.
FRENCH:	Amour de ma vie.
GERMAN:	Grosse Liebe.
ITALIAN:	Unico amore.
SPANISH:	Amor mio.

ENGLISH:	I dream of your kisses.
FRENCH:	Je rêve de tes baisers.
GERMAN:	Ich traume von Deinen Kussen.
ITALIAN:	Mi sogno i tuoi baci.
SPANISH:	Sueno con tus besos.

ENGLISH:	I love you.
FRENCH:	Je t'aime.
GERMAN:	Ich liebe Dich.
ITALIAN:	Ti amo.
SPANISH:	Te amo.

ENGLISH:	Will you marry me?
FRENCH:	Veux-tu m'épouser?
GERMAN:	Willst Du mich heiraten?
ITALIAN:	Mi vuoi sposare?
SPANISH:	Quieres casarte conmigo?

Valentine Fax

Lucretia Borgia was married four times before she was twenty-one.

Arturo Santora and Barbara Durante had the world's weirdest wedding. They married *at the bottom of the sea* in San Frutosis Bay, with everyone present dressed in deep-sea diving gear. The bride's bouquet was made of coral.

Mills & Boon sell twenty million romantic novels each year in Great Britain.

Brigham Young, the American Mormon leader, once married four women in one morning.

Vera Czemsk, a Prague housewife, jumped out of her sixth-floor bedroom window in 1967 after discovering that her husband was planning to leave her. She lived, however, and recovered in hospital – after landing on top of her runaway husband and killing him outright!

Poet W H Auden married the daughter of German novelist Thomas Mann to enable her to obtain a British passport. The first time they met was on their wedding day.

In one particularly romantic year – 1536 – Henry VIII's first wife, Catherine of Aragon, died; his second, Anne Boleyn, was beheaded, and he married his third, Jane Seymour.

♡ ✕ ♡ ✕ ♡ ✕ ♡ ✕ ♡ ✕ ♡ ✕ ♡ ✕ ♡ ✕ ♡ ✕ ♡

Romantic Tip No 3

Girls should never kiss with their eyes closed. It's always better to use your lips . . .

Roses are red,
Violets are blue,
Sugar is sweet,
So why aren't you?

Knock, Knock, Knock

Knock, knock.
– Who's there?
Lena.
– Lena who?
Lena little closer, I want to kiss you.

Knock, knock.
– Who's there?
Mary.
– Mary who?
Mary in haste, repent at leisure.

Knock, knock.
– Who's there?
Olive.
– Olive who?
I love you too, honeybunch!

Knock, knock.
– Who's there?
Iguana.
– Iguana who?
Iguana hold your hand.

Knock, knock.
– Who's there?
Vaughan.
– Vaughan who?
Vaughan day my prince will come!

Knock, knock.
– Who's there?
Honda.
– Honda who?
Honda the spreading chestnut tree . . .

Knock, knock.
– Who's there?
Moira.
– Moira who?
Moira see you, the more I love you . . .

Knock, knock.
– Who's there?
Donna.
– Donna who?
Donna sit under the apple tree with
anyone else but me . . .

Knock, knock.
– Who's there?
Sam and Janet.
– Sam and Janet who?
Sam and Janet evening, you will meet a
stranger . . .

Knock, knock.
– Who's there?
Aardvark.
– Aardvark who?
Aardvark a million miles for one of your
smiles . . .

Funny Valentines

What do a girl and a boy teddy bear do if
they love each other very much?
They go teddy!

What did the boy octopus say to the girl
octopus?
I want to hold your hand, hand, hand,
hand, hand, hand, hand, hand . . .

Why did the girl marry the acrobat?
Because he was head over heels in love
with her.

What salad do lovers prefer?
Lettuce alone.

'Why are you looking so upset?'
'When I asked Sally if I could see her
home, she said yes – and gave me a picture
of it.'

'What did your blind date look like?'
'Let's put it this way: she was better
looking over the telephone . . .'

How can you brighten up your boyfriend's
evening?
Sit with him in the dark.

'My girlfriend is like the National
Anthem.'
'Why's that?'
'She's stood me up more times than God
Save The Queen.'

'Did you hear about the couple who got married and went to live in a lighthouse? Their marriage is on the rocks.

ANN: 'I haven't had a single date all this week.'
SUE: 'I know, all your dates are married.'

'Beautiful girls don't bother me. I only wish they would.'

For twelve years Jim and Barbara were happy. Then they met.

ROSIE: 'I think the poorest people are the happiest.'
TOM: 'Then marry me and we'll be the happiest couple.'

CAROL: 'Do you remember when you proposed to me? I was so overwhelmed I couldn't speak for an hour.'
PETER: 'Yes darling, that was the happiest hour of my life.'

GARY: 'She swears she's never been kissed.'
DICK: 'That's why she swears.'

What is the happiest tree on St Valentine's Day?
The palm tree – because it has so many dates.

MARY: Am I the first girl you've ever kissed?'
ANDY: Maybe – your face looks familiar.'

Did you hear about the two vampires?
They loved in vein.

Say it with Flowers

1. Yellow Tulip = Hopeless love

2. Wild Daisy = I'll think about it

3. Violet = Faithfulness

4. White Lily = Purity and modesty

5. Pink = Boldness

6. Bramble = Envy

7. Primrose = Sadness

8. Purple Lilac = First emotions of love

9. Azalea = Temperance

10. Buttercup = Ingratitude

Knock, knock . . . knock, knock

Knock, knock.
– Who's there?
Saul.
– Saul who?
Saul over town you're in love with me.

Knock, knock.
– Who's there?
Congo.
– Congo who?
Congo on meeting like this.

Knock, knock.
– Who's there?
Toucan.
– Toucan who?
Toucan live as cheaply as one.

Knock, knock.
– Who's there?
Pyjamas.
– Pyjamas who?
Pyjamas round me honey,
hold me tight.

Knock, knock.
– Who's there?
Midas.
– Midas who?
Midas well have stayed at home for all you
care.

Further Funny Valentines

Did you hear about the manicurist who
married a dentist?
They fought tooth and nail.

How does a magician propose marriage?
'Will you be my wife, to halve and to hold?'

GIRL: Would you put yourself out for me?
BOY: Of course.
GIRL: Good. Then close the door as you go.

When is a room full of people empty?
When they're all married, because there's
not a single person there.

GIRL: I've heard an awful lot about you.
BOY: Maybe, but you can't prove it!

What is a bachelor?
A man who never Mrs a woman.

When does Cleopatra flirt?
When Julius Caesar.

DAUGHTER: Ben is awfully clever, Dad, he's got brains enough for two.
FATHER: Good, you'd better marry him then.

1ST WORM: I love you, I love you.
2ND WORM: Don't talk daft – I'm your other end.

1ST GIRL: I've proposed to three different men without avail.
2ND GIRL: Next time try wearing a veil!

1ST WOMAN: When I met my husband it was love at second sight.
2ND WOMAN: Not love at first sight?
1ST WOMAN: No, I didn't realise he was rich the first time.

1ST MAN: I'm worried about my daughter. She keeps being chased by the doctor.
2ND MAN: Has she tried an apple?

I'm going to marry a girl who can take a good joke.'
'That's the only kind you'll get.'

BRIDE: I have a confession to make. I can't cook.
GROOM: Don't worry sweetheart, I don't earn enough money to buy food anyway.

Roses are red,
Violets are blue,
So what went wrong
When they made you?

A Last Knock, knock

Knock, knock.
– Who's there?
Gwen.
– Gwen who?
Gwen will I see you again?

Knock, knock.
– Who's there?
Sincerely.
– Sincerely who?
Sincerely this morning I've been waiting
for my Valentine to arrive.

Knock, knock.
– Who's there?
X.
– X who?
X-tremely glad to get a Valentine from
you.

Knock, knock.
– Who's there?
Norma Lee.
– Norma Lee who?
Norma Lee I wouldn't send a Valentine,
but this year I'm in love.

Knock, knock.
– Who's there?
Sheik.
– Sheik who?
Sheik-speare married an Avon lady.

Knock, knock.
– Who's there?
Oliver.
– Oliver who?
Oliver, but she doesn't love me.

❤ ✕ ❤ ✕ ❤ ✕ ❤ ✕ ❤ ✕ ❤ ✕ ❤ ✕ ❤ ✕ ❤ ✕ ❤

Romantic Tip No 4

It is better to kiss a Miss than to miss a
kiss . . .

Romantic Riddles

Which girls should boys avoid?
Miss Chance, Miss Chief, Miss Hap, Miss
Take and Miss Fortune.

SUITOR: Sir, I want to marry your
daughter.
FILM STARLET'S FATHER: Can you
divorce her in the manner to which she has
been accustomed?

What did the ram say to his girlfriend?
I love ewe.

What would a cow use to write a Valentine
card?
A cattle pen.

Where did the cat have his Valentine
announcement printed?
In the mewspaper.

What made the rooster fall in love with the hen?
She egged him on.

How did the rooster propose to the hen?
He used fowl language.

Where did the two rabbits go after they got married?
On their bunnymoon.

How do Arab lovers dance?
Sheik-to-sheik.

What did Lady Hamilton say to Lord Nelson?
'You're the one-eye care for!'

'Will you marry me?'
'No, but I'll always admire your good taste.'

Happy St Valentine's Day!

From your Secret Admirer xxx